NIXON

The Rise and Fall of the President
at the Heart of the Watergate Scandal

Written by Sébastien Afonso
In collaboration with Thomas Jacquemin
Translated by Emma Lunt

History **50MINUTES**.com

RICHARD MILHOUS NIXON

KEY INFORMATION

- **Born:** 9 January 1913 in Yorba Linda, California.
- **Died:** 22 April 1994 in New York.
- **Political party:** Republican Party.
- **Election dates:**
  - 5 November 1968.
  - 7 November 1972.
- **Time in office:** Six years.
- **Main achievements:**
  - Ended American military involvement in Vietnam in 1973.
  - Improved diplomatic relations with Maoist China and later with the Soviet Union.

INTRODUCTION

Richard Milhous Nixon is undoubtedly one of the American politicians who provoked the most passion and hostility during the 20th century. He was brilliant and scheming, a paranoid liar: there is no shortage of adjectives and images to illustrate the complexity of this character. In collective memory, the name of the 37th President of the United States is of course still associated with the Watergate scandal that ended his political career.

Nixon's swift rise in the world of politics, after starting out with nothing, took place in a context of profound anti-communism. This anti-communism was closely linked to the Cold War (1945-1990), which he supported and which enabled him to stand out. When he became president, American society was suffering a serious crisis and was more divided than ever before.

His foreign policy as president was an undeniable success: he paved the way for détente (1962-1979) and, above all, he managed to put an end to American military intervention in Vietnam. Nevertheless, more questionable and unpopular situations tarnished his mandate, such as his involvement in the fall of Salvador Allende Gossens (Chilean president, 1908-1973) and, within domestic politics, the Watergate scandal.

Either way, his presidency marked a defining stage in American history and international relations.

BIOGRAPHY

CHILDHOOD, EDUCATION AND CAREER PATH

Richard Milhous Nixon, the 37th President of the United States, was born on 9 January 1913 in Yorba Linda, California, to a modest family. Originally from Ohio, his father, Frank Nixon (1878-1956), began as a tram conductor before starting a career in agriculture. He then opened a service station and a grocery shop in Whittier, a suburb of Los Angeles, before marrying Hannah Milhous (1885-1967), a devout Quaker. Nixon was the second of the family's five sons.

His education was marked by material deprivation and moral austerity. At school, he proved to be a bright and studious child, and an excellent speaker. He graduated from Whittier College (California) in 1934 and went on to Duke University (North Carolina, east coast), where he trained as a lawyer. He got his law degree in 1937. On returning to California, he was admitted to the bar and practiced law in Whittier for four years. It was during this time that he met Thelma Patricia Ryan (1912-1993), whom he married in 1940. They had two daughters, Tricia and Julie.

In 1942, the couple moved to Washington, where Nixon found a job in a federal organisation responsible for price control. Feeling unsatisfied by his professional situation, he joined the Marines that same year. Given the role of doing essentially administrative tasks, he did not have the chance to fight during the Second World War (1939-1945). He left the army, however, having reached the rank of lieutenant.

ENTRY ONTO THE POLITICAL SCENE

His career then took an unexpected turn. After his discharge at the beginning of 1946, he was contacted by the Republicans of California to represent them and to fight their Democrat adversary in the 12th district. After an aggressive campaign, he won the election. Elected as representative of California (1947-1951), he stood out thanks to his fierce anti-communism. His participation in the enquiry led by the House Un-American Activities Committee to find a former diplomat, Alger Hiss (1904-1996), guilty of espionage to help the Soviet secret service, earned him a certain notoriety.

On 7 November 1950, Nixon was elected Senator of California, and was then appointed Vice-President of the United States the following year, alongside President Dwight David Eisenhower (1890-1969). Accused of embezzling electoral funds into his own pocket, he managed to justify himself and the matter was not pursued. Re-elected in 1956, he became the de facto leader of American politics following the president's illness. In 1959, he went to Moscow, where he debated the respective virtues of capitalism and communism with the Soviet leader Nikita Sergeyevich Khrushchev (1894-1971).

He was the Republican presidential candidate in the 1960 elections, but was beaten by the Democrat John Fitzgerald Kennedy (1917-1963). Two years later, he suffered another defeat when he stood for Governor of California, and he decided to take a temporary break from politics.

A televised debate between Nixon and his presidential opponent, John F. Kennedy.

PRESIDENTIAL ELECTIONS AND RESIGNATION

Having returned to being just a corporate lawyer on Wall Street, he managed to slowly rebuild his political foundations. After being chosen as the Republican candidate once again for the presidential election of November 1968, he defeated his opponent, Democrat Hubert Horatio Humphrey (1911-1978), by promising voters that he would quickly end the Vietnam War. Nevertheless, the United States' involvement in the conflict continued until 1973.

The campaign of 1968.

It was, above all, in international affairs where Nixon obtained good results, particularly with the signing of a treaty with the USSR in 1972 regarding nuclear weapons, and with the beginning of diplomatic relations with Communist China.

After being easily re-elected in 1972, he was shaken by the Watergate scandal. Revelations of the wrongdoing of his administration threatened his career. Forced into a corner, he resigned on 8 August 1974. He was replaced by his vice-president, Gerald Rudolph Ford, Jr. (1913-2006) who granted him immunity for all the crimes committed during his presidential terms. The Watergate scandal did not, however, dismiss Nixon from the American political scene entirely. In fact, at the end of the 1970s, he was still going on many trips, particularly to China and the USSR. He also wrote several works, including his memoirs, before dying from a heart attack on 22 April 1994 in New York.

POLITICAL, SOCIAL AND ECONOMIC CONTEXT

THE SIGNIFICANT SOCIAL CHANGES OF THE 1960S

American politics in the 1960s was marked by the federal interventionism of Democratic presidents, who launched large social reform projects. In his inauguration speech following his election in 1960, John F. Kennedy told Americans that he would push back a 'new frontier' (which refers to the American myth of the frontier in the conquest of the West), a frontier of prejudices and poverty. It was only after JFK's assassination in Dallas on 22 November 1963, however, that Lyndon Baines Johnson (1908-1973), who became president, expanded these social reforms. During his presidential term (1963-1969), he had Congress adopt the programme of equal rights and social justice started by his predecessor. This desire for change and progress was part of his ambition to establish a 'Great Society'.

Within this context of economic growth, Lyndon Baines Johnson's Great Society consisted of a programme of particularly ambitious legislative and social reforms that led to:

- The implementation of laws to protect civil rights, the Civil Rights Act (1964), which banned any type of discrimination in public places and services, and the *Voting Rights Act (1965)*, which guaranteed black people access to the ballot box.
- The start of the fight against poverty, notably in terms of

health. The president created a public health system (July 1965) with Medicare aimed at older people and Medicaid to deal with the medical care of the poorest in society.
- The rise of social expenditure between 1960 and 1965. The education system received government aid, as did housing and culture.

This welfare state policy saw significant results by firstly contributing to the reduction of poverty. Nonetheless, despite a positive economic situation, conservatives strongly criticised the State's involvement by denouncing the exorbitant cost of these measures. Yet, from 1967, the Vietnam War dominated debates and hindered reforms.

AMERICAN SOCIETY IN TURMOIL

Paradoxically, while these ambitious social changes were being drawn up, the American society of the 1960s was experiencing a serious identity crisis. The foundations of the American way of life were subjected to social, cultural and ethical criticisms.

GOOD TO KNOW

The expression 'American way of life' refers to a model of society that was established and reached its peak during the 1950s, when the United States was experiencing a period of prosperity and unprecedented economic growth. Referring to both a lifestyle and the aspiration to be happy, the American way of life is characterised by an attachment to material success and to the consumer goods that come with this (cars, suburban houses, household goods, etc.). As a result, a certain consensus and ideological conformism associate individual success with unrestrained consumerism.

At the end of the 1950s, black people in America paved the way for protest by fighting against social segregation and for equal civil rights. The theme of Black Power became increasingly widespread, as did the exaltation of black culture ('Black is beautiful'). Some movements, such as the Black Panther Party (an African-American revolutionary movement founded in California), which was created in 1966, broke away from non-violence. Against a backdrop of poverty and segregation, riots took place in the ghettos of large cities between 1964 and 1968:

- The Watts Riots in the suburb of Los Angeles in 1965, which occurred following an unremarkable incident between a black man and a white policeman, caused 34 deaths and over 1000 people were injured. The significant damage was estimated to have cost 40 million dollars.
- In Nashville (Tennessee) and Houston (Texas) in May 1967, a revolt arose in over 110 towns and reached its peak in Newark and Detroit in July, where the riots killed 300 people.
- After the death of Malcolm Little, known as Malcolm X (American politician, 1925-1965) in February 1965, leader Martin Luther King (American pastor, 1929-1968) was assassinated on 4 April 1968. The news provoked a wave of violence around the country.

The unrest, which was initiated by the struggle of black people, progressively spread to other ethnic minority groups. After many strikes and a national grape boycott, the Chicanos (Americans of Mexican origin), who were the main employees in the wine-making sector, forced large agricultural companies to negotiate with the Union of Farm Workers, the union of Californian agricultural workers and grape pickers. American Indians created the American Indian Movement in 1968 and carried out an increasing number of dramatic actions to gain recognition of their culture and their oppression. They thus symbolically occupied the island of Alcatraz for 19 months starting in November 1969.

The awareness of social injustice accompanied the politicisation of young people. With almost eight million students at the end of 1960s, universities became hotbeds for protest. One notable example of this is the appearance of the New Left movement at universities. Among its leaders was Herbert Marcuse (1898-1979), a philosopher who criticised American capitalist society as much as the Soviet communist regime. In 1962, this movement was replaced by groups such as the SDS (Students for a Democratic Society) whose ideology was composed of a mixture between anarchism and pacifism, socialism and Marxism, etc. The anti-establishment climate on campus was amplified in October 1964 with the Free Speech Movement, which originated at the University of California, Berkeley.

From 1965, the escalation of the Vietnam War and the introduction of conscription (military recruitment based on being called to a contingent) helped increase the number of people supporting the student protests. At the same time, young people developed an anti-conformist culture which helped in the movements' success.

GOOD TO KNOW

Counterculture is characterised by the rejection of the conformism of American society in the 1960s. It was first embodied in literature by writers such as Allen Ginsberg (1926-1997) and Jack Kerouac (1922-1969) – who represent the Beat Generation – then moved towards celebrating drugs, sexual freedom and art. Hippies, who promoted, among other things, non-violence and community living, are the best symbol of this movement.

Finally, women's protests also gradually emerged. In her work *The Feminine Mystique*, sociologist Betty Friedman (1921-2006) expressed the social alienation that women suffered. In 1966, she founded, along with other intellectuals, the NOW (National Organization of Women) in order to denounce sexual discrimination, campaign for contraception and gain the right to abortion.

FROM DÉTENTE TO STALEMATE IN THE VIETNAM WAR

The international context in the early 1960s was marked by major crises such as the construction of the Berlin Wall on 12 and 13 August 1961 and the Cuban missile crisis in 1962.

The latter led the two superpowers, the USA and the USSR, to endeavour to avoid direct confrontation. While it did not put an end to the Cold War, it did mark the beginning of a period of relative pacific coexistence.

The Space Race that brought the two superpowers into conflict henceforth went in the United States' favour. America, which had formerly been left behind by the Soviet Sputnik satellites, succeeded in getting the first manned space vehicle into orbit in 1962 and putting the first man on the moon – Neil Alden Armstrong (1930-2012) became the first man to walk on its surface on 21 July 1969.

But the situation in Vietnam became American society's main concern. Due to their lack of foresight, the United

States had become bogged down in a deadly and unpopular war, isolating the Americans on the international scene. Loyal to their doctrine of holding back communism, they supported the authoritarian regime of South Vietnam against communist North Vietnam. A national liberation front, which was created in 1960 and composed of Marxists and nationalists, then engaged in an armed battle.

American headquarters were unaware of the war which was playing out on a national level, did not boil down to a simple anti-communist fight, and would involve prolonged effort, with no territorial aim and with no clear way out. The Vietnam War attracted barely any attention from American public opinion before 1965:

- After helping the French during the First Indochina War (1946-1954), in 1955, the Americans promoted the rise to power of Ngo Dinh Diem (1901-1963), a profoundly anti-communist Catholic, in South Vietnam.
- In 1960, the situation in Vietnam declined with the pro-gressive recapture of the south by North Vietnam, led by Ho Chi Minh (1890-1969), but the conflict remained marginal and was still little known by the majority of Americans.
- Nevertheless, the number of American military advisers involved continued to increase. While there were only 700 advisers in 1961, this number reached 3 200 one year later and 12 000 at the end of 1962. At the time of John F. Kennedy's death, South Vietnam had 16 000 advisers.

The Gulf of Tonkin Resolution, voted by American Congress in August 1964, marked a true turning point in the war. In response to the North Vietnamese torpedo boat attacks that were launched against an American destroyer (the *Maddox*) on 2 and 4 August, President Lyndon Baines Johnson was granted the freedom to react with force by Congress, without voting for a declaration of war. The intervention was immediate:

- Starting from March 1965, the Americans opted to launch operation 'Rolling Thunder', which consisted of an intensive bombing campaign against North Vietnam and aimed to destroy military infrastructures and to hinder the support given to communist forces in the South.
- As the massive bombings did not yield the expected results, the number of young Americans involved began to rise, going from 23 000 men in 1964 to 536 000 in 1968. Nevertheless, American forces remained inferior in number to the South Vietnamese forces.

On the ground, they were involved in a war of attrition in which it was difficult to distinguish mere citizens from Viet Congs. Mixed within the local population or hiding in inaccessible zones, American forces could not get a decisive victory, while planes bombed the north of the country incessantly, using a diverse and destructive arsenal (napalm, defoliants, fragmentation bombs and chemical weapons).

RISING OPPOSITION

As the involvement of American forces continued, protests grew denouncing what seemed increasingly like a 'dirty war'.

Opposition to the Vietnam War grew and the number

of peaceful protests increased. The implementation of conscription in 1965 in order to recruit new troops provoked discontent among the young people mobilised and their families. Moreover, young people from privileged backgrounds who bypassed the recruitment system were blamed.

Nonetheless, before the end of 1967, surveys showed that over 60% of Americans supported the president's policies, refusing the humiliation of a retreat. But as the war effort increased, losses became more significant and media coverage of the conflict intensified, pacifist protest movements became more aggressive.

On 30 January 1968, which was the start of the Lunar New Year, the 'Tet Offensive' was launched by the Viet Congs and the North Vietnamese on around 100 towns and cities including Saigon (today known as Ho Chi Minh City). This general offensive showed the vulnerability of the United States and their South Vietnamese allies. Doubt arose within the administration regarding a quick victory, particularly on 31 March, when President Lyndon Baines Johnson announced that they were ceasing to bomb the North and beginning negotiations.

Even if the economic rise did not seem threatened on the eve of the presidential electoral campaign of 1968, the United States seemed far from where they had been ten years previously: conformism was being questioned, society seemed more sceptical than ever about the decisions taken and, above all, the country was stuck in a distant war that was dragging on.

A meeting between Lyndon B. Johnson and Nixon, 26 July 1968.

THE POLITICAL AGENDA OF 1968

On 5 November 1968, the Republican Richard Milhous Nixon was elected president with a weak majority, beating the democratic candidate Hubert Horatio Humphrey, who gained the vast majority of African-American votes.

The inauguration of Nixon on 20 January 1969.

The Vietnam War, the unrest of pacifist demonstrations and racial riots were all factors that divided America. Listening to what he called the 'silent majority', Nixon emphasised his political experience with an agenda that he hoped would reassure public opinion, which was worried by the troubles and resistant to the surrounding permissiveness.

He successfully convinced the white middle class, which was made up of farmers, traders, employees, civil servants and skilled workers, who remained on the outskirts of protest movements. In order to reach these 'forgotten' Americans, he developed an electoral programme based on two main ideas: order and prosperity. It was on these themes and the so-called threat to American values that he planned to win over his electorate and to criticise the policies that had been carried out until then:

- He criticised the way Democrats had led the Vietnam War. He promised to end the war that was dividing American society, as well as to find an honourable exit route from the war and to give the country its international foundation back.
- He denounced the expensive and unsuccessful social reform projects that his predecessors established and particularly stigmatised the intervention of the State, which had caused inflation.
- In favour of restoring order, he denounced the excesses of the policy of integrating ethnic minorities, which had only led to violence.

As president, however, Nixon faced a Democratic Congress which held a majority in the Senate and the House of Representatives. Victorious in the elections of 1968, but also in those of 1970 and 1972, the Democrats left the Republican administration little room for manoeuvre.

PRESIDENTIAL TERMS AFFECTED BY ECONOMIC CRISES

From the start of his first term, Nixon inherited a delicate situation, marked by a decline in the American economic situation. The main source of worry came from the progressive increase in unemployment, which reached 6% in 1970. The economy certainly remained prosperous, but pessimism reigned.

First and foremost, the president had to deal with a budget and trade deficit. Already from the start of the 1960s, the American balance of payments (an equation that calculates the total value flow between a country and foreign countries) displayed a deficit caused by tax reductions, military expenses and foreign investments. These problems, associated with the threat of inflation, led the new president to change his economic positioning:

- In order to halt the crisis, he adopted a liberal and monetarist policy (1969-1971) which involved slowing the growth of money stock while gradually reducing budgetary expenses.
- Growing inflation (between 6 and 8% per year) and the budgetary deficit (which reached 23 billion dollars in 1971) had a direct effect on the balance of payments. The recession began in 1971 and ruined any attempt to balance the budget. From then on, the American economy found itself facing significant stagflation (economic stagnation that is associated with inflation).
- Nixon then adopted a more Keynesian economic revival

policy which led him to put an end to the dollar's convertibility into gold and to leave the American currency to float, subjecting imports to a 10% surtax and locking in prices and salaries.

Despite these measures, inflation persisted and even reached 8.8% in 1973, the dollar continued to lose value and growth came to a halt.

The situation recovered slightly in early 1972, as announced by Henry Kissinger (American political scientist and diplomat, born in 1923), thanks to an imminent peace agreement in Vietnam which explains Nixon's triumphant re-election in November 1972. Indeed, he received 61% of the votes, or a majority of 17 million people. Following his re-election, he found himself facing a deteriorating economic situation once again. But he was unable to stop the rise of prices or rising unemployment which reached 7.2% in 1973.

The petrol shock of 1973 was an exogenous crisis that hit the United States. The Yom Kippur War (October-November 1973), an Israeli-Arab conflict, led countries in the OPEC (Organization of the Petroleum Exporting Countries), who were favourable towards the Arabs, to implement a petrol embargo between October 1973 and March 1974. From then on, the price of petrol skyrocketed. Paradoxically, this energy crisis was favourable to the United States, but revived inflation in Europe. From 1974, the dollar climbed back up, allowing commercial balance to be restored.

THE PRESIDENT'S SOCIAL AND REGULATORY POLICY

Nixon did not break away significantly from the social policies implemented by his Democratic predecessors, contrary to the position he appeared to express during his 1968 campaign. Having benefited from the votes of those who advocated a reduction in the State's involvement, social spending nonetheless increased seven-fold during his presidency.

On 22 January 1970, during his State of the Union Address, he revealed his project for a 'new American revolution', which referred to a collection of measures regarding medical insurance, environmental protection and the redistribution of government financial aid within the United States. Some successful measures included:

- a significant increase in social spending on older and underprivileged people;
- the creation of the OSHA (Occupational Safety and Health Administration) in 1970 in order to respect laws aimed at guaranteeing the safety and security of workers;
- he implemented a series of ecological laws and the creation of the EPA (Environmental Protection Agency).

Nevertheless, his project was reduced to only its most significant measures. In order to redirect the interventionism inherited from the Great Society, he suggested implementing the FAP (Family Assistance Plan), a social reform plan guaranteeing a minimum annual income to all the poorest working families. This meant ending the aid which benefitted only black people and other minorities in order to help all underprivileged people. Yet, facing the double opposition of conservatives and liberals, his project failed and he was forced to abandon it in 1972.

Furthermore, the president wished to redirect part of the federal subsidies to social security. In his State of the Union Address on 22 January 1971, he suggested establishing a new, decentralised federalism in order to share revenues between states and municipalities. Although his project was unsuccessful, he still managed to pass the Revenue Sharing Act on 20 October 1972, which left a small part of the subsidies granted by Washington available to the states for five years.

Facing the issue of minorities, Nixon did not impede civil laws on desegregation. Beyond his desire to establish 'black capitalism' (a desire which was realised in March 1969 by the Office of Minority Business Enterprise, which aimed to encourage minorities to become involved in commercial activity), the president adopted a low-profile attitude (known as benign neglect), in order to avoid any social turmoil. Regarding the issue of integration, Nixon's administration remained hostile towards bussing, which involved mixing black and white students in schools by transporting them on school buses.

Far from seeming to be a fanatical conservative, he was more like a Republican with centrist, even progressive, policies in terms of social issues.

THE STRUGGLE OF LEAVING
THE VIETNAMESE MESS

After rising to power in January 1969 with no clear plan, Nixon was looking for an honourable way to withdraw American forces while protecting South Vietnam from the attacks of the North. Despite his promises to end the war quickly, he was actively engaged in continuing it and secretly approved the bombing of suspected Viet Cong bases in Cambodia, which was officially neutral, in March 1969. Moreover, the contingent that was sent to the frontline increased until, in April 1969, there were 543 000 men there. These measures led to a decrease in his popularity.

It was only in July 1969 that Nixon began the de-escalation with a so-called 'Vietnamization' of the conflict strategy. This meant gradually substituting American troops with South Vietnamese forces, who had been previously equipped and trained as required. This indirect assistance enabled the reinforcement of South Vietnamese troops while continuing with the progressive withdrawal of American forces on the ground.

In the United States, pacifist and student movements continued to put pressure on the government until the ceasefire and the abolition of conscription in June 1973:

- More than 250 000 people campaigned in Washington against the Vietnam War on 15 October 1969.
- In April 1970, the invasion of Cambodia provoked a revolt on almost 400 campuses. On 4 May, an enormous riot at Kent State University (Ohio) killed four people. Faced with this increasing violence, Congress was forced, in July 1970, to abolish the Gulf of Tonkin Resolution of 1964.

Many other scandals also mobilised public opinion against the State and increased opposition to the war. Massacres committed by American soldiers in My Lai (in northern South Vietnam), which were revealed by the press 18 months after they occurred, were hidden by the government. Furthermore, in June 1971, the *New York Times* published secret files, the Pentagon Papers, despite the president's attempts to censor the press. These files showed that Congress and the public had been deceived regarding the reality of American involvement in Vietnam. It became clear that the Gulf of Tonkin incident had been manipulated.

This climate of protest contributed to accelerating negotiations. Nixon entrusted his National Security Adviser, Henry Kissinger, with the mission of making contact with

North Vietnam's representative, Le Duc Tho (1911-1990), but made sure to keep quiet about it. Negotiations concluded on 28 January 1973 with the Paris Agreement which ended American involvement. In Vietnam, the truce lasted only two years before North Vietnamese forces began their offensive once again in March 1975. Without American support, South Vietnam collapsed and the capital, Saigon, fell on 30 April.

A FOREIGN POLICY MARKED BY DÉTENTE

Rivalry with the communist world developed and Nixon pursued the détente process that had been started several years earlier.

There was then a spectacular strategic turnaround regarding China. Indeed, Kissinger suggested making America the mediator in a new triangular relationship with China and the USSR. The president made this strategy, which played on the disagreements between China and the USSR, his own, as the latter was unable to let Sino-American relationships developing without reacting. Nixon's official visit to Beijing in February 1972 and his meeting with President Mao Zedong (1893-1976) marked a significant diplomatic step.

The results of this outreach strategy paid dividends. Aided by the American president's visit to Moscow in May 1972 and that of Leonid Ilich Brezhnev (1906-1982) to the United States in June 1973, relations with the Soviet Union improved. Dialogue between the two superpowers was guided by a linkage strategy (which involves connecting files between each other and making concessions on one area in order to receive returns on another). Regarding nuclear arms, the USSR and the United States symbolically signed the first SALT (Strategic Arms Limitation Talks) agreement regarding the limitation of strategic weaponry on 26 May 1972, while trade relations sorted themselves out.

Nixon, however, remained loyal to his anti-communist beliefs, leading the United States to support dictators and repressive political regimes:

- He supported the military dictatorship in Greece and supported to overthrow of the archbishop, Makarios III (Cypriot prelate and statesman, 1913-1977) in 1974.
- In Chile, the socialist regime led by Salvador Allende Gossens, who was democratically elected, was unsettled. The American president was directly involved in the military coup d'état organised on 11 September 1973 by General Pinochet (Chilean officer and statesman, 1915-2006), who benefitted from the help of the CIA. During this military coup, Allende committed suicide.

Despite undeniable diplomatic successes, these affairs tarnished the president's image around the world.

THE PRESIDENTIAL POWER CRISIS: THE WATERGATE SCANDAL

The 1972 campaign, which led to Nixon's triumphant re-election, was also the starting point for a major scandal that called the institution of the presidency into question. On 17 June 1972, five men – who were initially believed to be burglars – were arrested by the police inside rooms belonging to the Democratic Party in Washington, at the Watergate hotel. Equipped with microphones for spying, it quickly became clear that this team, which was responsible for installing a system to illegally listen to conversations, was made up of former CIA agents who were associated with the CRP (the Committee for the Re-election of the President).

An enquiry by two *Washington Post* journalists, then a senatorial fact-finding mission in April 1973, revealed that many figures from the president's circle were directly involved in the affair. It was also discovered that Nixon recorded all the conversations that took place in his office in the White House. When he was ordered to hand over the tapes in order to determine whether he was connected to the Watergate scandal, he refused by invoking his executive privilege. But the noose tightened around the president as the enquiry progressed:

- The investigation revealed the illegal actions of the tax office, the FBI and the CIA against their opponents. Resignations and accusations were rife among the president's close collaborators.
- Although he had no proven connection to the Watergate scandal, vice-president Spiro Agnew (1918-1996) was affected by tax fraud affairs and was forced to resign in October 1973. Nixon replaced him on 6 December 1973 with Gerald Rudolph Ford, who was then the House Minority Leader.
- In July 1974, the Supreme Court ordered the president to

give the tapes to the select committee.

- At the same time, the House of Representatives began an impeachment process against Nixon, accusing him of obstruction of justice, abuse of power and contempt of Congress.

Nixon is forced to share transcripts of the tapes

Little by little, American public opinion turned against their president. His popularity plummeted, going from 70% in 1973 when he signed the peace agreement in Vietnam to just 24% in April 1974. Facing the imminent impeachment process, Nixon resigned on 8 August.

IMPACT

FOREIGN POLICY – NIXON'S TRACK RECORD

Without a doubt, it is within the domain of foreign policy that Nixon, with the help of Henry Kissinger, obtained the most tangible results. Indeed, he established détente thanks to his getting diplomatically closer to China, the normalisation of relations with the USSR, the US's mediation of the Yom Kippur War, and of course the end of the Vietnam War in 1973.

Handling the Vietnam War was undoubtedly the main difficulty that Nixon had to deal with during his presidential terms. The cost of this war was enormous:

- On a human level, 58 000 Americans died and 300 000 were injured, as well as almost one million Vietnamese.
- The cost of the war (160 million dollars) dangerously weakened the dollar.
- The moral and psychological consequences were significant. Young Americans returned weakened by the conflict, particularly the 'Viet-vets' (Vietnam veterans) who did not receive a warm welcome on their return to the United States.

It was therefore American society as a whole that was traumatised by the war: anti-communist consensus was shattered and the citizens' trust in their institutions crumbled. The effects of this Vietnamese ordeal were felt just as much within the United States as outside and led to the revision of American policy throughout the entire world. The United States lost their credibility with their allies and their power was seriously weakened, even more so two years after the signing of the peace agreement when, on 9 March 1975, the North Vietnamese launched an offensive against South Vietnam. When Gerald Rudolph Ford called on Congress to help Saigon, he was forced to accept defeat in the face of the hostility of the senators. On 30 April 1975, the North Vietnamese captured the city and Vietnam was reunified under communist control.

Furthermore, the success of the détente strategy did not last long. It peaked in August 1975 with the signing of the Helsinki Accords, which brought together 35 countries, including the United States and the USSR. These agreements led to the recognition of the European borders which stemmed from the Cold War, as well as economic cooperation between the East and West, but also the commitment of the USSR to respect human rights. Nonetheless, relations between the two superpowers quickly diminished following the installation of nuclear missiles in Europe in 1977, then with the USSR's military intervention in Afghanistan two years later.

THE PURSUIT OF A SOCIAL AND CIVIL LEGACY

Although more discreet, Nixon's results in domestic politics had lasting influence within the domain of social policy and civil rights. Far from breaking with the policies of the welfare state, social costs increased considerably: from

1970 to 1976, the social security budget doubled. Although they were reduced, these social aid and local redistribution projects proved to be truly progressive all the same.

It should be noted that within the social domain, the president had to face the Supreme Court that acted as a political and judicial counterweight. From 1969, the Burger Court, in which four judges out of the nine that make up the court were selected by Nixon, proved to be rather conservative. In June 1971, they directly opposed the president by defending the principal of freedom of press, defined by the First Amendment of the Constitution, during the Pentagon Papers scandal. They also distanced themselves from the president's position by legalising bussing and even abortion in January 1973.

In terms of civil rights, clear advances were recorded, even if Nixon was happy just to validate the reforms made by his predecessors:

- desegregation in Southern schools continued, going from 68% of black schoolchildren attending segregated schools to just 8% in 1972;
- his administration supported the positive discrimination policy voted for under Lyndon Baines Johnson in favour of ethnic minorities and women;
- finally, ethnic and racial unrest which had continued throughout the previous decade faded.

LESSONS LEARNED FROM THE VIETNAM WAR AND THE WATERGATE SCANDAL

The shock caused by the Vietnam War and the Watergate scandal cast doubt on the status of the president and led to the affirmation of checks on their power. The Second World War, the Cold War and above all the Vietnamese conflict contributed to the strengthening of executive power. Nixon's election in 1968 followed this path, and even accentuated this process of 'presidentialisation', particularly within the domain of foreign policy. Nevertheless, the Vietnam War and the Watergate scandal emphasised the dangers of what American historian Arthur Meier Schlesinger (1917-2007) called 'imperial presidency'.

On an institutional level, legislative power took its revenge even before the Watergate scandal. Congress repealed the Gulf of Tonkin Resolution in 1970. Two years later, they demanded that they be given every document relating to the security of the State and, above all, they decided to stop the bombing of Cambodia in June 1973. Finally, the adoption of the War Powers Act, which highlighted the rights of Congress and limited presidential power in the use of the armed forces, was a real humiliation for Nixon. Legislative power took back a role that had been taken from them.

Finally, the media played an essential role that could thereafter no longer be denied. Televised reports revealed to Americans the tragedies and uncertainty of the war and televised hearings of the Watergate Committee mobilised public opinion against Nixon. This scandal, which was a real personal crisis of a president who had been led astray, but also a major political crisis for the presidential institution, finally proved the constitutional stability of the United States.

SUMMARY

1913
9th Jan.: Birth of Richard Milhous Nixon

1947
Entry onto the political scene

1955
Start of the Vietnam War

1969
20th Jan.: Inauguration as
37th President of the United States
21st July: Neil Armstrong walks on the moon

1973
20th Jan.: Second inauguration
28th Jan.: Withdrawal of American
troops from Vietnam

1973-1974
Apr.-July: Watergate Scandal

1974
8th Aug.: Resignation

1994
22th Apr.: Death of Nixon

- Richard Milhous Nixon, who was born to a modest family and was a trained lawyer, made his blazing ascent into politics and stood out with his profound anti-communism.
- In November 1968, he won the presidential elections with a small majority over his Democratic rival. He benefitted from the support of the white middle class, who were tired and worried by the unrest that affected society. This 'silent majority' also expected the new president to withdraw American troops from the Vietnam War.
- From the start of his presidential term, he was faced with an unpleasant situation which was marked by budgetary deficits, rapid inflation and rising unemployment.
- He led a centrist social policy, which earned him criticism from both conservatives and liberals.
- His triangular diplomacy divided socialists while paving the way towards détente.
- In November 1972, Nixon was re-elected. He owed his triumphant re-election, in part, to the announcement of an imminent peace agreement in Vietnam.
- The Paris agreements, which were signed on 27 January 1973, established a ceasefire and the total withdrawal of American troops. The cost of the Vietnam War for the American side was heavy: 58 000 dead and 300 000 injured.
- Following the Watergate scandal and facing the threat of an impeachment process by Congress, Nixon became the first American president to resign from his duties on 8 August 1974.

We want to hear from you!
Leave a comment on your online library
and share your favourite books on social media!

FIND OUT MORE

BIBLIOGRAPHY

- American Council of Learned Societies (1999) *American National Biography*. New York/Oxford: Oxford University Press.
- Coppolani, A. (1997) *La vie politique aux États-Unis de 1945 à nos jours*. Paris: Ellipses.
- Durpaire, F. (2013) *Histoire des États-Unis*. Paris: PUF.
- Fohlen, C. (1988) *Les États-Unis au XXe siècle*. Paris: Aubier.
- Kaspi, A. (1986) *Les Américains. Les États-Unis de 1945 à nos jours*. Paris: Seuil. Issue 3.
- Kaspi, A. (1983) *Le Watergate*. Brussels: Éditions Complexe.
- Kaspi, A. and Harter, H. (2012) *Les présidents américains. De Washington à Obama*. Paris: Tallandier.
- Lacroix, J-M. (2009) *Histoire des États-Unis*. Paris: PUF.
- Mélandri, P. (1984) *Histoire des États-Unis depuis 1865*. Poitiers: Nathan.
- Mélandri, P. and Portes, J. (1991) *Histoire intérieure des États-Unis au XXe siècle*. Paris: Masson.
- Mourre, M. (1996) *Dictionnaire encyclopédique d'Histoire*. Paris: Bordas.
- Nouailhat, Y-H. (2009) *Les États-Unis de 1917 à nos jours*. Paris: Armand Colin.
- Portes, J. (1992) *L'histoire des États-Unis depuis 1945*. Paris: La Découverte.
- *Larousse* (No date) *Richard Milhous Nixon*. [Online]. [Accessed 24 January 2014]. Available from: <http://

www.larousse.fr/encyclopedie/personnage/Richard_
Milhous_Nixon/135374>

ADDITIONAL SOURCES

- Aitken, J. (1996) *Nixon.* Washington: Regnery Publishing.
- Ambrose, S. E. (1989) *Nixon: The Education of a Politician 1913-1962.* New York: Simon & Shuster.
- Black, C. (2007) *Richard M. Nixon. A Life in Full.* New York: PublicAffairs Books.
- Hoff, J. (1994) *Nixon Reconsidered.* New York: Basic Books.
- Nixon, R. (1979) *Memoirs.* London: Arrow.

ICONOGRAPHIC SOURCES

- A televised debate between Nixon and his presidential opponent, John F. Kennedy. © Associated Press.
- The campaign of 1968. © National Archives and Records Administrations.
- A meeting between Lyndon B. Johnson and Nixon, 26 July 1968. Royalty-free reproduction picture.
- The inauguration of Nixon on 20 January 1969. © Oliver F. Atkins.
- Nixon is forced to share transcripts of the tapes. Royalty-free reproduction picture.

FILMS AND DOCUMENTARIES

- *David Frost Interviews Richard Nixon.* (1977) [Documentary]. Jørn Winther. Dir. USA: David Paradine

Productions.
- *Nixon.* (1995) [Film]. Oliver Stone. Dir. USA: Cinergi Pictures Entertainment.
- *Richard Nixon: Man and President.* (1996) [Documentary]. Alan Goldberg. Dir. USA: ABC News Production.
- *Reputations: The Secret Life of Richard Nixon.* (2000) [Documentary]. Paul Tilzey. Dir. UK: British Broadcasting Corporation.
- *The Assassination of Richard Nixon.* (2005) [Film]. Niels Mueller. Dir. USA/Mexico: Anhelo Productions.
- *Frost/Nixon.* (2008) [Film]. Ron Howard. Dir. USA: Universal Pictures.

IMPROVE YOUR GENERAL KNOWLEDGE

IN A BLINK OF AN EYE !

www.50minutes.com